MY CENTENNIAL DIARY
A Year in the Life of a Country Boy

by Earll K. Gurnee
Skaneateles, New York, 1876

New York History Review Press
Elmira, New York

My Centennial Diary - A Year in the Life of a Country Boy
by Earll K. Gurnee, 1876
transcribed by Diane Janowski

Published by New York History Review Press
Elmira, New York

For the latest on New York History Review, please visit
www.NewYorkHistoryReview.com

Copyright © 2009 Diane Janowski

This book was designed and laid out in Adobe InDesign using typeface Adobe Garamond Pro.

Notice of Rights. All rights reserved. No part of this book may be reproduced or transmitted in any form by any means, electronic, mechanical, photocopying, recording or otherwise, without the prior written permission of the author. For more information on getting permission for reprints and excerpts, contact us through our website.
www.NewYorkHistoryReview.com

ISBN: 978-0-578-02985-6

First Edition

for Minnie

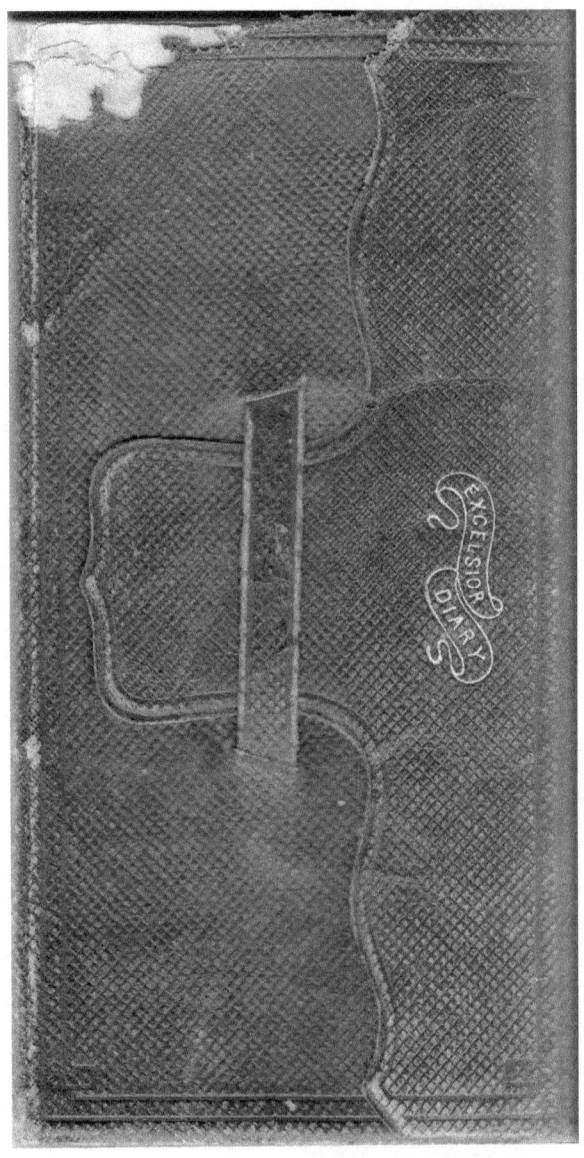

Earll's diary in its current condition. Courtesy of the Eleanor Barnes Library, Elmira, New York.

Table of Contents

Foreward..8

Maps of Skaneateles and area............................10, 11

People in the Diary..12

Map of the Town of Sennett................................15

My Centennial Diary...17

Map of Willow Glen...44

Map of Mottville..51

Centennial Notes..81

Bibiliography..82

Afterward...84

Foreward

In our *Learning from History* series of Upstate New York diaries, accounts of young people's lives on the farm, or in the home, help us to understand their thoughts and experiences. Each narrative offers a unique perspective on teenage life in rural New York, and serves as an important primary resource in the study of American history.

My Centennial Diary is the journal of 18-year-old Earll Kilbourne Gurnee of Sennett, New York - two miles from downtown Skaneateles. Earll was born on January 28, 1858 in Madison, Wisconsin, the son of Robert and Lucy Ann (Kilbourne) Gurnee. The family moved to New York in 1863 to be closer to his grandparents Caleb and Cynthia Brown on West Lake Road in Skaneateles, New York. When he was sixteen, Earll's parents purchased a farm on Franklin Street Road.

Beginning on January 1, 1876, Earll recorded the events of his life in a small 3 x 5¾ inch pocket diary with one entry to the page in very nice handwriting. Earll's notations were confined to the spaces allotted and are written in pencil or ink. His handwriting is mostly legible, except for a few names or places that cannot be deciphered. Earll's spelling is left as he spelled it. Clarifications have been added in brackets. The photographed pages from his diary are actual size.

Earll lived with his parents and little sister Rose. He had plenty of friends and neighbors. He was generally very happy in his life – he enjoyed his family, going to school, and afterschool activities. He attended the Skaneateles Academy. Earll was a very hard worker on his family's farm. In his words he exclaimed love for unobtainable Florence, his "angel without wings", a young woman of twenty-four. She is mentioned in his diary, sometimes just as "F" or "her." Earll's other girlfriend was Sally/Sarah .

My Centennial Diary invites us into the daily life of a New York teenager, through his own words and experiences. We hear Earll's voice as he shares his joys, sorrows, and enthusiasm for life in a rural farming community.

The Eleanor Barnes Library acquired Earll Gurnee's diary in 2008. So far as is known, this transcription is its first published version.

Diane Janowski, Publisher
New York History Review

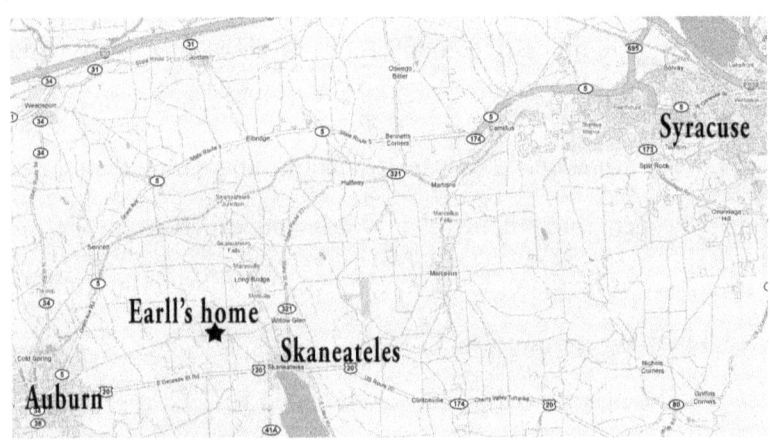

Earll's home is about two miles from downtown Skaneateles and twenty-two miles from Syracuse. Right: map of Skaneateles and surroundings from *Atlas of Onondaga County, New York*, 1874. Steele Memorial Library, Elmira, New York.

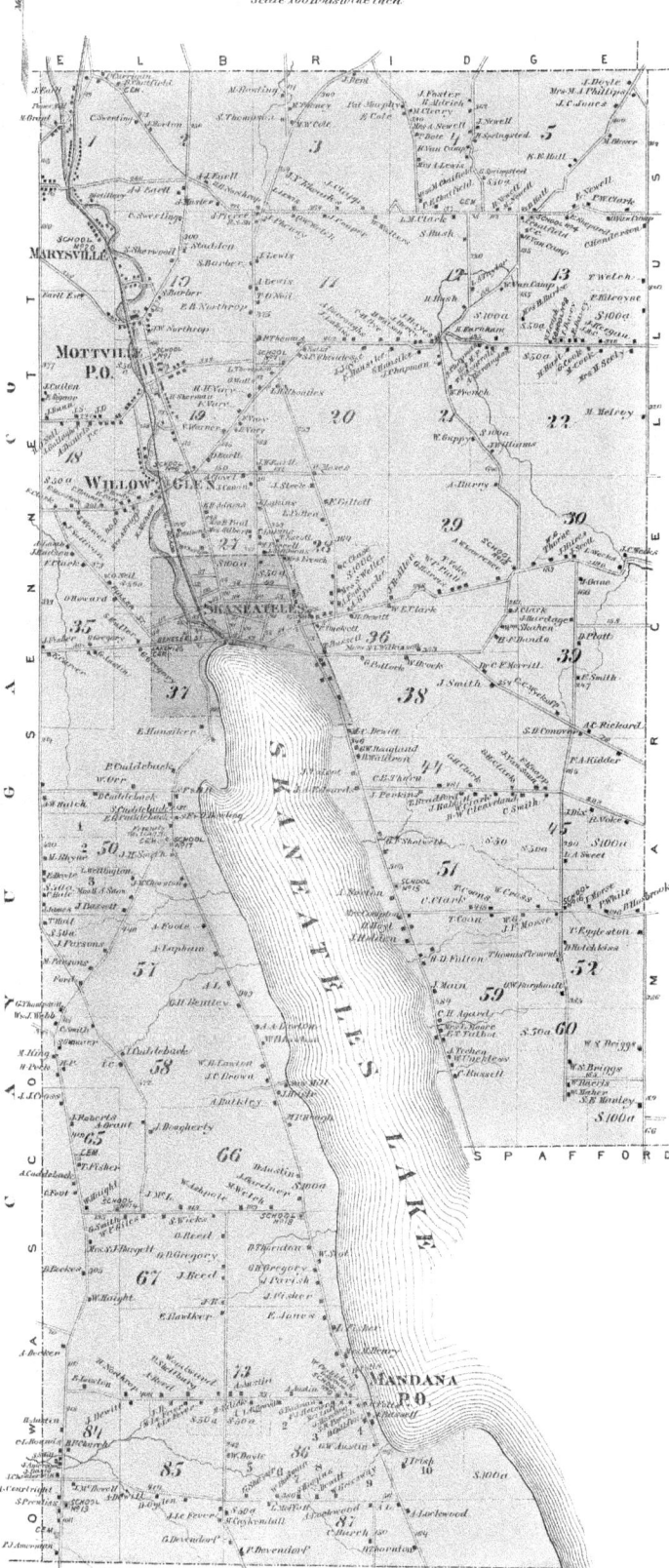

People in this Diary

Earll's family in 1876

Mother - Lucy, age 44
Father - Robert, age 51, farmer
Rose - sister, age 3

Friends, Neighbors, and Relations

Charley Abbott - age 20, lived in Niles, New York
Fannie Beardslee - new teacher after the old teacher gets arrested
Mark Browne
Carrie Brown
Dr. George Campbell - physician in Skaneateles, New York
Mr. Chase
Chauncey Clark - age 12, son of Edwin
Millie Clark - age 18, daughter of Edwin
Edwin Clark - age 56, farmer in Skaneateles, New York
Mr. Clift - owned farmed to the north
Mr. H. Colby
Mr. Daniels
Mr. and Mrs. Devit [George & Mary Dewitt] lived next door to Barney Hall in Niles, New York
Deuels
Harrison Dodge - Skaneateles *Democrat* newspaper editor - age 64
Addie Durston - neighbor, age 22
Will or Bill Durston - neighbor, age 25
Jim Durston - farmer, age 48
Charley Earll - classmate, age 16
Johnny Elliot
Uncle Emmett Dewitt [Stephen E.]- age 68, married to Mira [Mariah]

F - his beloved Florence Gardner, age 24
Fun - family horse
Thomas Gardner - Florence's father
George - his favorite horse
Mr. Gillett - sometimes spelled Jilled
Mr. Goodwin
Grandma - [paternal] (Electa Gurnee) lived in Cottage Grove, Wisconsin
Grandpa - [maternal] (Caleb Brown) lived in Elbridge, New York
Barny Hall - (Barney) lived in Niles, New York next door to the Dewitts
Hattie - aunt
W. Harry
Fred Hutson
Mr. Hutson - next door neighbor
Mr. Huxford
Jed [Jeddiah] Irish - man who drowned, age 44, lived in Skaneateles, NY
Cousin Isaac
Cousin Sam Gurnee from Wayne, New York
Jack - family horse
Jennie - Aunt Jennie
Jim - new family horse
Frank Jones - lived at the farm just to the east
Will Jones
Fred [or F. L.] Kilborn Kilborne Kilbourn
W.M. or Willis Kilborn Kilborne Kilbourn - cousin
Wilbur Lawton
Edd Ludwig
Mira Dewitt [Mariah]- age 66, aunt married to Emmett [Stephen E.],
    lived on Cream Hollow Road, in Niles, New York
Mooley - family cow
Thomas O'Flaherty - farmer, age 53, lived two farms to the west
Mr. and Mrs. Powell - lived across the road
Edd [Powell] - age 26, lived across the road

Frank Powell - age 23, lived across the road
Irving
Gabe
Albert
Mr. Irving Rhoades
Jim Roots
Sally/Sarah - girlfriend, last name unknown
Miss Hattie Scribbens - seamstress
Mr. [Milton] Shaver - farmer, age 56
Charley Signor - age 27
Mr. Smith - lived on Franklin Street in Skaneateles, New York
Mr. and Mrs. Spaulding
Stevenson - newspaperman
Uncle Alex Gilmore - age 26 - farmer in Sennett, NY, married to Addie
Aunt Addie [Adelaide] Gilmore - age 28
May and Gilmore - related to Alex Gilmore
Uncle George and Edith
Uncle Jonathan
Uncle Oliver
Uncle Sylvester Tilscomb
William Sampson - man with a problem
Charley Thompson - classmate
Jakob Waldron - farmer, age 46, lived in Sennett, New York
Wallace
Mr. Weaver
Job Weeks - lived next door to the school
George Wilson - neighbor lived down the street
Professor Wright - the school teacher

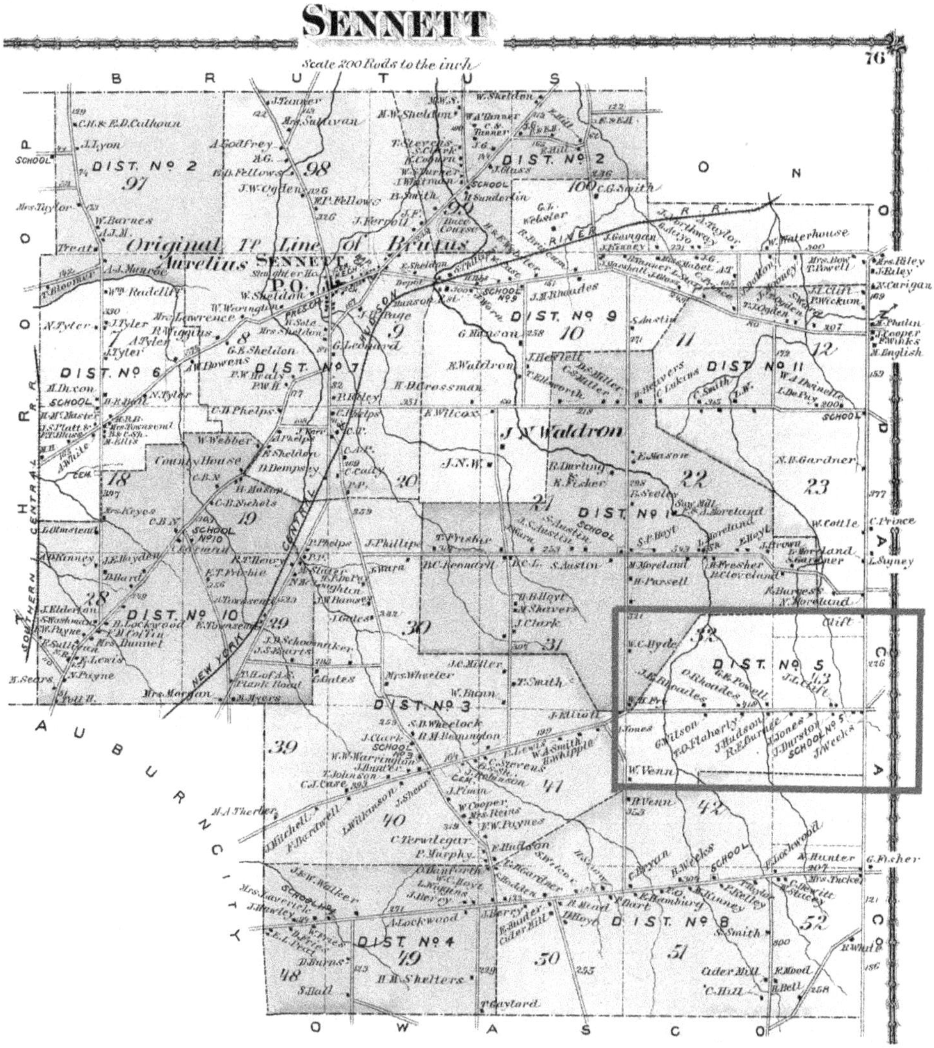

SENNETT

Above, town of Sennett, NY. Right, close up of Franklin Street Road where the Gurnee family lived. *1875 Cayuga County map*, Steele Memorial Library, Elmira, NY.

JANUARY,   SATURDAY 1.   1876.

The morning opened dark and Foggy. but not cold. Mud from ½ to 2 feet deep. toward noon the weather cleared and the balance of the day was exceedingly fine and warm Thermometer 60° Throughout the day At 12 last night the centennial was ushered in with ringing of bells and and shouting and screeching from many voices. Many business places was illuminated That is to say Wallaces, Foot & N.4? Allis & Halls I.S[amuel] & Son Stores A large amount of Whiskey was probably consumed as many were Hilarious and a few in a pugilistic. In fact I deemed it imprudent to leave the vicinity of the Store for fear of violence and consequently paid O'Grines one dollar to stay the night

Warren Wallace

MY CENTENNIAL DIARY

January, Saturday 1. 1876.
The morning opened dark and foggy, but not cold. Mud from ½ to 2-feet-deep. Toward noon the weather cleared and the balance of the day was excruciatingly fine and warm. Thermometer 60 degrees throughout the day. At 12 last night the Centennial was ushered in with ringing of bells and shouting and screeching from many voices. Many business places were illuminated. A large amount of Whiskey was probably consumed as many [people] were hilarious and a few pugilistic. In fact, I deemed it imprudent to leave the vicinity of the store for fear of violence and consequently paid O'Grimes one dollar to stay the night.

January, Sunday 2. 1876.
School commences tomorrow after a weeks vacation - which spent sawing wood. Pa plowed yesterday and I plowed day before yesterday in the big meadow.

January, Monday 3. 1876.
I went to school today – had to walk for Pa plowed. Week ago today we sawed down an elm tree which measured 100 feet up to where the longest limb was 6 inches. Through it was about 4 feet through where we sawed it off and made five logs about 12 [feet] long.

January, Tuesday 4. 1876.
Attended school today – had pretty good lessons. It has frozen up and I walked to school. The roads are dreadful rough.

January, Wednesday 5. 1876.
I sapose I must write something as I did not have any diary until several days of the new year had passed away. I have to "think up" what has passed and all I can remember is that I went to school. I went down to the schoolhouse and heard the spelling "nine" practice. [A spelling bee played in baseball terms – as in nine players on a team.] Chauncey Clark is the champion. He is also catcher. Edd went home with F which made me fearful jealous.

January, Thursday 6. 1876.
Examination commenced today. I was examined in Arithmetic the first thing in the morning. There were 8 examples all of them quite easy. I omitted two of them for want of more time. In the afternoon I was examined in Algebra – five questions and five examples was all that was given. I guess I answered all of them correct.

School closed at half past two.

Will Durston's spelling nine from Willow Glen and Edd Powell's nine from our own district meet for a spelling contest tonight. I am to be "scorer."

January, Friday 7. 1876.
Examination continued today. I was examined in Grammar – do not believe I "passed." I was also examined in Reading and Spelling. I was pronounced "excellent" which is next to the highest. 100 words were pronounced in Spelling. I returned two library books (one for myself and one for F. Powell) and got two more viz *Seek and Find* and *Palace & Cottage*. Edd won the prize last night although Will's nine made a good show. Addie Durston was "pitcher." I scored with the aid of Charley Signor. I found it quite a job but an interesting one. Edd's side spelled 3 words more than Will's in eleven innings. Mr. and Mrs. Devit went up [down] to Cream Hollar today [Cream Hollow Road, Niles, New York]. Emmett came down after them. Bought this diary today for ½ price at Wallace's.

January, Saturday 8. 1876.
Well, today has been a workday. It rained this afternoon quite smart. Pa and I put new eaves and inners on the stow boat. We sawed them out of elm planks. It was quite a job. Mr. Hutson got 25 pounds of white flour today – he paid 85¢ for it. I have just finished *Palace & Cottage* – it is a good book. I read the other one through last night. I expect to be "scorer" down to Willow Glen some time next week. It still rains at 9 o'clock.

January, Sunday 9. 1876.
Today is warm but rather gloomy. I went over to Mr. Powell's [house across the street] this morning. Edd paid me 40¢. The thermometer has averaged 50 degrees all day. It rained some this afternoon. I ought to write a composition tonight, but I don't believe I shall. Tomorrow is school and I am glad of it. Pa got a letter from Uncle Sylvester. Frank Powell brought it up. Uncle Sylvester's people were all well. He enclosed $10 to pay subscription for *American Agriculturalist* which I must not forget tomorrow.

January, Monday 10. 1876.
It froze some this morning and I went to school horseback on George [horse]. I mailed a letter for Edd P., two for Millie Clark and two for Father. Paid Wallace 50¢ and paid subscription for *American Agriculturist* for Uncle S.

And I was tardy in the bargain. The report for examination was read, but I was not in time to hear my Grammar report.
Arithmetic 6 1/4 (perfect is 8)
Algebra 10 (perfect is 10)
Reading 7 1/2 (perfect is 8)
Spelling 84 (perfect is 100)
Grammar 4 4/10 (perfect is 10)

It is fearful cold tonight. The thermometer is 15 degrees. The wind is west. It snows a little. H was over this evening. The wind blind-slammed at the schoolhouse and took out 8 panes of glass.

January, Tuesday 11. 1876.
Attended school as usual – the weather is pretty cold. I went a-horseback. Professor Wright whipped the boys today – one of them tripped the Prof up and brought him to his knees. I went down to the schoolhouse tonight and pronounced words for the "nine." Edd had a bad cold and could not talk plain enough. Handed in my composition today – subject "Hunting." The deepest sounding is 8¾ miles. The greatest height ever reached by a balloon is 6 miles.

January, Wednesday 12. 1876.
We thrashed our clover down at Mr. Clift's – we had one bushel. Seward's clover thrasher did the job. I walked to school today. It snowed about 3 inches and if the roads were smooth there would be [a] little sleighing. I killed a muskrat tonight out west of the horse barn – he was a nice one. I went down to the schoolhouse again tonight – there were seven boys down there – we had quite a spell. I spelled 18 out of 23. Edd, Irving, Fred, Gabe, Albert and I had a splendid game of "tag" at our gate after the "spell" although it snowed hard and the wind blew strong from the west.

January, Thursday 13. 1876.
I rode to school with Frank Jones. Had pretty good lessons although I did not feel very well on account of having a hard cold. Thermometer 2 degrees above zero. Rehearsed my piece to the Professor today. Went down to Willow Glen to score at the spelling match. Will Jones also scored. Will Durston won by an excess of 105 over 77. Will's = 82, Edd's = 77. I think it was a cooked job and am not alone in my opinion. After the match the nine on both sided spelled down. Chauncey Clark spelled the longest "Bully for Chan."

January, Friday 14. 1876.
Attended school – rode with Frank. I spoke my piece this afternoon. I returned two library books and got three viz *Frank in the Woods, Starry Flag first book* and *Outward Bound*. It snows fine tonight – had to walk home from school. We all went over to Mrs. Powell's – had a very good visit. We went over to supper. Edd is very indignant at the way we were treated down to Willow Glen. I don't blame him one bit. Will ought to have his ears cropped. Paid Mr. F--- $1.36 - 25¢ is still due him to make $1.61.

January, Saturday 15. 1876.
It has been quite warm today. Father went to the Village with the stow boat and got 292 lbs of coal this forenoon. I finished *Frank in the Woods* today – it is a splendid book. We did not do hardly any work today.

Father, Mother, Rose, Mr. and Mrs. Powell, Mr. and Mrs. Spaulding all went up to Mr. Wilson's tonight [3 farms to the west]. Father drove up with the Hutson's bobs [bobsleighs] and carried all the visitors along. Fred came over this evening. I read *Starry Flag* through this evening – it is "strong." It is quite warm tonight – I guess it does not freeze much. I am sorry – I am afraid it will all break up again.

January, Sunday 16. 1876.
It has thawed all day, but has not stormed any. My head has ached pretty steady. I read *Outward Bound* through. I forgot to write yesterday that Pa bought a bushel of turnips. News is rather scary today and I guess I shall have to shut up shop for tonight. I forgot to say that I found a silver 20¢ piece today.

January, Monday 17. 1876.
I went down to school with the buggy and got to school just in time to escape being tardy. I took a lot of harness for Uncle Emmett. Aunt Hattie started for Delaware County today on the 10:40 train. I went over to Mr. Powell's a little while this evening and found out that the little cluster of stars in a row high in the Southeast is Orion's belt and the three at the right and a little below is Orion's sword.

January, Tuesday 18. 1876.
I went down to school in the sulky and had rather a wet time of it, for it rained quite considerably off and on. I took a piece up to Dodge for Edd to put in the paper about the spelling school. The thermometer stands at 54 degrees tonight and the south wind blows a gale. I went over to Mr. Powell's a little while tonight. Got a postal card from Cousin Isaac today. They expect to come out here in about two weeks.

January, Wednesday 19. 1876.
I went to school in the sulky – it was awful muddy – had pretty good lessons. It rained like suds this afternoon. We had extemporaneous composition tonight – there were fine subjects – I took the subject "Our Centennial" – I wrote 131 words.

A hole may be bored in a piece of glass with a three cornered file if the point of friction be kept wet with spirits of turpentine.

Nitric acid corrodes on steel and is therefore used to write on steel.

January, Thursday 20. 1876.
I tried it a-foot today – got along first rate - it froze some last night – but not enough to hold. One of the students fired off a firecracker in school today. Professor Wright could not find out who it was but I found out who it was – it was Wilber Lawton.

January, Friday 21. 1876.
I walked to school again today – took back my library books today. We had Mathematical exercises today instead of Compositions. Prof made Roscoe Giles and I stay after school and pick up all the waste paper on the floor – it was not fair as we had hardly any and several other students had five times more than we. I got *Shamrock and Thistle*, *Make or Break*, and *The Cruise of the Frolic*. Got a letter from Hattie – she was to start at 3 o'clock this morning and get to Albany at 7 and at Alex's at 11 o'clock.

January, Saturday 22. 1876.
It snowed some today, but not enough to make sleighing. Pa fixed my fine boots. Fred Hutson and I sawed a lot of wood. Mother put a large plaster on my back which has been very lame lately.

January, Sunday 23. 1876.
It thawed today quite a little. I went over to Mr. Powell's today and had a lot of butternuts, and a piece of pie for lunch. Was ashamed of staying so long. Frank's butternuts made him sick. Mr. and Mrs. Powell came over here this evening. Sarah was over here a little while tonight.

January, Monday 24. 1876.
Walked to school with Frank Jones – had pretty good lessons considering who studied them. Rode home with him. Durston stopped at the schoolhouse. Edd was riled up considerably and I don't blame him after

what Bill Durston put in the *Free Press* calling Edd a sore head. But Edd is a-going to give it to him in *The Democrat* this week. I'll bet Bill will read it over more than once. By gum.

Fred H. was over here this evening a little while. I traded gloves with him, and gave him a "Dime Novel" to boot.

January, Tuesday 25. 1876.
Walked to school again today – or rather part of the way and rode the rest with Edwin Clark. Had a lot of errands to do viz screws, glass, rubber.

I heard that Aunt Mira fell down stairs and hurt her some – but nothing serious. It snowed like everything tonight, but the thermometer is almost too high (28 degrees) for a good run of sleighing.

Frank Jones is over here after Arithmetic help in "ratios."

Dancing School Masquerade Ball tonight.

January, Wednesday 26. 1876.
Walked to school again as usual. Weather about as usual. Lecture at the academy tonight – subject "Temperance and Staid-Life in New York." Went over to Mr. Powell's tonight. Edd's reply to Bill Durston in *The Democrat*, which I took down to Dodge, speaks well for the writer.

We almost went to Syracuse.

January, Thursday 27. 1876.
It rained last night and covered everything with ice half an inch thick. Went to school in the cutter – much against my wishes. Rained also when I went to school but did not get much wet. F. Jones rode with me. Well, it thawed some all day consequently had to drag home through the mud about as I expected. Saw Mrs. Duel [?]. Mira fell down the cellar stairs and blackened her eyes, hurt her shins and her back. Went over to Mr. Powell's again tonight and collected my library books so not to forget them tomorrow. Bought some things at Wheadon's.

January, Friday 28. 1876.
I hitched George on Mr. Jones' buggy to ride to school. Frank, of course, rode with me. Returned my library books and got three more. *Dungeon and Escape* is one of them. It rained almost all day. Fred Hutson and I went down to the Village and attended the Masquerade Ball. It was first rate. There were about 45 masked. There were several very nice costumes – both gentlemen and ladies. There were very few that I knew. Got home a few minutes after twelve.

There were 3 very nice tableaux viz "Bandits waiting for their Victim," "The Bandit's Death," and I don't know the name of the other.

January, Saturday 29. 1876.
I did not get up until after seven o'clock. It was quite warm this morning, but it gradually grew colder until at dark it was frozen hard enough to hold out. Father and I cleared out the corn-house and made it a little more comfortable for the hens. Mr. Hutson got 146 lbs of hay today. My back has been very bad today. I guess I have caught cold and it has settled there. I wish if it has it would move.

January, Sunday 30. 1876.
It froze up pretty solid last night. Father and Mother and Rose went over to Uncle Jonathan's today. I stayed at home. Edd Powell came over a little while this afternoon. My eyes commenced to get sore tonight and the light hurts them.

Frank Powell got our mail today. He brought a letter from Cottage Grove [Wisconsin]. Grandma is quite sick, and she has been so for 5 months.

January, Monday 31. 1876.
Did not go to school today on account of my eyes. Father went to Auburn today. The roads are rather rough. He took out seven dozen of eggs. I went over to Mr. Powell's and from there to Mr. Spaulding. Their baby is sick – a hard cold on the lungs. Mother put on a potato poultice tonight.

February, Tuesday 1. 1876.
Walked down to school with Frank Jones. Mailed a letter to Aunt Hattie. The potato poultice did the business for my eyes – they are not very bad today. Came home by way of the Brigg's Woods in good season. Went over to Mr. Powell's again tonight. Mrs. Powell, Frank and Edd went off some where with the team, but Edd came back after they had gone a little way. The boys are down on Mr. Powell's pond skating. I wish I was down there.

February, Wednesday 2. 1876.
Walked to school again today. It was very stormy and blustery. The schoolhouse was very cold and there were 2 or 3 panes of glass broken out. Prof omitted the morning exercises to allow us more time to warm. The wind was west and we had a rather rough time getting home.

February, Thursday 3. 1876.
Attended school. The thermometer was 2 degrees below zero this morning – about 16 degrees tonight. Prof got mad and broke a pointer over Edd Ludwig's shoulder this afternoon. I borrowed a watch off W. Harry and have it in my pocket now.

Got *Breaking Away* by H. Clary and have just read it through. Also *Shoo Fly*. Bought a box of collars today – no. 13 1/2.

February, Friday 4. 1876.
Attended school. Walked down with Frank. Stopped at the schoolhouse and Frank had an argument with Edd about punishment in schools. Edd holding that a teacher could punish scholars as much as he thought necessary as long as he did not endanger life or limb. Frank holding that a teacher had no right to strike a scholar with a ruler and make "black and blue spots." Edd says that a teacher can, if the trustee stands by him, punish a scholar with a ruler and make "black and blue spots" if necessary. Frank is pig-headed and too unreasonable to argue with.

February, Saturday 5. 1876.
Went to the woods and rolled up there large elm logs in the afternoon.

Father and Albert sawed and I split quite a pile of wood. Mr. Jilled came after with a sleigh he got about 1000 lbs of hay I guess.

Weather very fine – sun shining all day. Thermometer ranged about 20 degrees.

February, Sunday 6. 1876.
Weather quite warm – thermometer about 45 degrees tonight. The Hutson boys came over here and we had lots of fun playing "Sheep in the Pen." I went over to Mr. Powell's tonight – had a good time talking to Edd.

The *Tree Press* correspondent has broke out in a new spot. He is a soft chap and an Irishman to boot – his name is O'Hara.

February, Monday 7. 1876.
Attended school. Hitched George on to Mr. Jones's buggy. It thawed all day and the roads are pretty good.

Prof Wright gave me a card on which was printed that 20 unexcused marks suspends one from school a whole day. I have 11 marks against me. Mailed a letter for Edd. Thermometer about 45 degrees tonight.

February, Tuesday 8. 1876.
Attended school. Got a letter from Cottage Grove saying Grandma was dead and Uncle George married Edith. I also got a letter from Uncle Victor Colby enclosing a money order of $25. Cousin Isaac and wife arrived here today. Pa brought them from Auburn. Grandma died on January 29, 1876. Uncle George was married two weeks before.

February, Wednesday 9. 1876.
Attended school – went down in the sulky. It froze last night quite hard. Edd gave me 3 quarters this morning but did not find out who sent them.

It rained most all day. I consequently got rather wet. Got our mail. Dodge put in Grandma's death [obituary] in *The Democrat*. [She was originally from Skaneateles.]

Earll's signature and address from the first page of the diary (larger than life size).

February, Thursday 10. 1876.
Went to school in the sulky. It froze almost hard enough. Examination today. I was examined in Arithmetic in the forenoon and Algebra in the afternoon. School closed at 11 o'clock in the forenoon and at 2:20 in the afternoon for those who had nothing further to do.

Cousin Isaac and Father went down to the Village today. I went into Eckel's bakery with them. They have a very nice engine – the name is the Economizer. They were making crackers.

February, Friday 11. 1876.
Went to school – it rained all day pretty near. Examination continued. I got two more library books viz *Two Years before the Mast* and *Young America*.

It was a nasty bad day. Frank Jones did not go to school today nor yesterday. Went over to Mr. Powell's.

February, Saturday 12. 1876.
Cousin Isaac, me and Sally went up to Barny Hull's, and Pa went to bring back the horse. The sun shone all day. I done the chores and that was all. Pa got back about 6 o'clock. Can't think of anymore to write – except that I have been over to Mr. Powell's.

February, Monday 14, 1876
Examination.
Arithmetic = 9 (perfect = 10)
Algebra = 4 (perfect = 10)
Reading = 10 (perfect = 10)
Spelling = 76 (perfect = 100)
Grammar = 7 (perfect = 100)
Total   = 108
[January 10 examination]   = 103 3/10
                                     4 7/10 gain

Attended school – but was tardy on account of the bad wheeling – it rained some – the mud is knee-deep.

February, Thursday 10. 1876.

Went to school in the sulky. It froze almost hard enough to bear but is rather poor ice. Examination to day I was examined in Arithmetic in the forenoon and Algebra in the afternoon. School closed at 11 oclock in the forenoon and at 2.30 in the afternoon for those who had nothing further to do. Cousin Isie and Father went down to the village to day I went in to Eckel's bakery with them they have a very nice engine the name is the Economizer they were making crackers

FEBRUARY, WEDNESDAY 16. 1876.

Snow drifts in every direction. Rode to school with Frank Jones we went by the way of the Willow Glen the snow was 5 feet deep on Clarks hill we came very near being stuck. Prof. had us write all we could think of about what had happened at school so far this week. Charley Thomas let the cat out of the bag by writing that he ran away. I just came home from the Powells

I found a large double gentleman's shawl in front of John Hutson's this morning.

February, Tuesday 15. 1876.
Went to schoolhouse – it snowed quite hard – and continued to do so all day. The west blew quite hard making it rather hard traveling horseback – about a foot of snow fell I guess. The steamboat "Ben H. Porter" dragged anchor or rather the ice carried it off towards the head of the lake.

The talk is that they are all a-going to build a new side-wheeler soon. I hope they will.

I just came home from Mr. Powell's.

February, Wednesday 16. 1876.
Snow drifts in every direction. Rode to school with Frank Jones – we went by way of Willow Glen – the snow was 5-feet deep on Clark's Hill – so we came very near to being stuck.

Prof had us write all we could think of about what had happened this week. Charley Thompson let the cat out of the bag by writing that he ran away. I just came home from Mr. Powell's.

February, Thursday 17. 1876.
Weather a little colder – went to school. J. Jones took Frank Jones and I down.

I gave Stevenson an advertisement to put in his *Free Press* about the shawl.

Frank Powell was over here a little while this evening. The sleighing is rather good, considering.

February, Friday 18. 1876.
Went down to school with Frank Jones's cutter. The speaking and com-

positions were good. I changed two library books. Frank Jones and I took a ride around the Village.

Frank Powell told me that Oscar Howard was the owner of the shawl I found.

February, Saturday 19. 1876.
We broke a road up to the woods and drawed down two loads of wood. Took down a little hay for my horse about 5:00.

Uncle Emmett was down – he came over here and got his bobs and some traps.

Mira and the children came also.

February, Sunday 20. 1876.
Father and Mother went to up the Village today to see Emmett's folks. It snowed some today. I made a stove pipe for Fred Hutson. Our folks heard that a woman by the name of Masters was found Saturday morning with her throat cut from ear to ear.

February, Monday 21. 1876.
Drove Jack [horse] to the Village – school closed early on account of a strong smell that came from the furnace. Went down to Lawson's, John Biler's, and Briggs. Pa drawed home from Gillett's brick yard two small loads of tile – 525 tile by count.

February, Tuesday 22. 1876.
Washington's Birthday. There was no school. Pa went down to the Village and got Mr. and Mrs. Devit. I went hunting at noon. Frank Jones went with me. We hunted our woods but did not get anything nor see anything. We came through O'Flaherty's dooryard on our way home – he has 14 head of the snottiest cattle I ever saw together. I went over to Mr. Powell's this evening. Edd and I had a good time talking about cattle, marrying, and religion.

February, Wednesday 23. 1876.
Walked down to school with Frank Jones. The weather was rather rough. Thermometer 8 degrees tonight. It is about 6 degrees above zero. Great Centennial/Washington's Birthday Party and supper at Jim Roots last night. Frank Powell was King William. Prof Wright was George Washington. We had a bad time coming home tonight.

February, Thursday 24. 1876.
School did not commence until 9:45. Regents examination in Arithmetic was the first thing -10 examples.

In the afternoon, Grammar, 80 questions 2½ hours. I omitted about 15 questions in Grammar.

Went over to Mr. Powell's tonight. Played several games of Euchre with Frank.

February, Friday 25. 1876.
School did not commence until 10 o'clock as yesterday. Second session in Arithmetic lasted until noon. In the afternoon was Geography and Spelling. There was 100 words in spelling.

February, Saturday 26. 1876.
Drawed one little log to mill. We could not load the big ones on a pair of bobs. They were so high and the room was as small. We worked all the afternoon trying to load one but did not succeed.

February, Sunday 27. 1876.
I have been sick most of day with a cold. I have just written a letter to Cousin Fred. We also wrote one to Aunt Jennie.

February, Monday 28. 1876.
Drove Jack down to school today. Frank rode with me. Everything went on quiet. Albright had the kindness (!) to allow me the pleasure of changing a library book. I got Fenimore Cooper's *Pioneers*. Pa, with the help of Mr. Powell, got out the logs and took one to mill.

February, Tuesday 29. 1876.
Drove Jack today also. Pa drew the other logs to mill. I guess he had a hard time. Sleighing continues to be good. Ice cutting is going on every Saturday with great vigor.

March, Wednesday 1. 1876.
Walked to school today with Frank Jones. A couple more inches of snow fell last night. Sleighing splendid. Father took a load of hay out to Auburn today – he got $11. He had 1030 pounds. He brought back a load of manure.

March, Thursday 2. 1876.
Walked to school. Pa went out to Auburn and got another load of manure.

Prof told Charley Earll to stay after school and then somebody whispered so loud that Prof heard them and he thought it was Charley grumbling, so Prof called him up and tried to lick him, but Charley would not be punished for what he had not done, so they had a lively time, and Charley got some pretty hard knocks, and Mr. Waller [a lawyer who lived nearby] interfered and Prof held up his horns, and Charley went down to show Dr. Campbell his bloody neck and hand.

March, Friday 3. 1876.
Walked down to school as usual with Frank Jones. The excitement not yet abated in regard to Charley Earll. Everybody is against Professor Wright. He was arrested at 9:00 o'clock this morning by M.V. Dewitt. There was an examination at 11 o'clock at Dewitt's office. School closed at 2:30 today. Frank Powell visited the school today.

March, Saturday 4. 1876.
Father went to Auburn with a load of hay – he took 1090 lbs. He brought back a bench for $1.75 and a plow point.

I did not do anything but the chores. Went up to the swamp to shoot rabbits with Fred H. We did not see any, but we heard them however. It thawed some today.

March, Sunday 5. 1876.
Very pleasant today – thawed like fine all day. Sleighing all gone. Grass or mud. I read stories most all day. Went over to Mr. Powell's a little while this evening.

March, Monday 6. 1876.
Rode down to school in the sulky. Sleighing all gone. Wellington spoke this morning. Mr. Hutson drew some hay home.

Man loves little and often.
Women much and rarely.

March, Tuesday 7. 1876.
Went to school in the sulky this morning. Mud getting rather deep. I got down to the Village 7:45. The earliest of any morning I have been down to the Village. Frank Jones put his horse in Mr. Daniel's barn without a license. Prof Wright is bound over to appeal at County Court. Pa went down to the Village today. Mr. Hutson got some straw today. It rains quite hard tonight. I have just come from Mr. Powell's.

Money is like manure – of very little use except when spread.

March, Wednesday 8. 1876.
Went to school horseback. I met the train. George bucked almost under them. Frank Jones must also put his horse in Mr. Daniel's barn.

March, Thursday 9. 1876.
Walked down to school. Next week is examinations. Wednesday and Thursday. I got some cards today but they are most all gone among the boys. I have got one back from most of them - 20 pink cards 10¢.

March, Friday 10. 1876.
Walked to school today. I got some more cards – fancy ones 8 for 10¢. They are for G---. Mr. Goodwin broke down again today by Root's Corners. Frank Jones got rather mad at me tonight. Pa and E. Durston trimmed apple trees this afternoon.

March, Saturday 11. 1876.
I ditched some today out by the pond under the willow trees. E. Durston and Father trimmed trees this afternoon. It rained some this forenoon. I got a letter from Fred Kilborn today.

March, Sunday 12. 1876.
It was rather cool today. Fred Hutson is working down to Mr. Shaver's. He came over here today. Edd brought a pile of Boulie's magazines. There are a lot of good stories.

March, Monday 13. 1876.
It froze some last night and snowed some. I walked to school and so did Frank. It was fearful cold coming home because we had to face a strong west wind.

March, Tuesday 14. 1876.
Walked to school again. It is froze harder than it was yesterday but it is not so cold. Will Durston visited the school today. Scholars are rather rude but there is not many here today. I took John Durston's gun home this morning.

March, Wednesday 15. 1876.
Examination today. I had Arithmetic today but ran way in the forenoon because there was nothing for me to do. The examinations did not amount to much in my eyes. There were quite a lot of visitors. I got Hattie at Willow Glen on the 4:20 train. Uncle Alex and Aunt Addie and May are well and last but by no means, Cousin Gilmore a week and one day old.

March, Thursday 16. 1876.
Weather rather stormy. I did not go down to examination. Pa took Hattie up [down] to the Village. I did not do much – weather rather squally.

March, Friday 17. 1876.
We drew out horse manure – 17 loads. Stormy weather but not cold. We got 8 bushels of bailed white spring wheat for seed.

March, Saturday 18. 1876.
Very cold and stormy - we put up 18 bushels of oats and 6 of corn and took them to Mottville on Hutson's bobs. Sleighing very good. Mr. Powell has got a sick cow.

March, Sunday 19. 1876.
Thermometer 4 degrees about zero – did not do anything all day – except a little sleighing.

March, Monday 20. 1876.
Father went down and got the grist in the forenoon. Snowed like everything this afternoon. I carried 95 pounds of hay out [to] the horse barn today.

March, Tuesday 21. 1876.
Good sleighing. Father went to Auburn with 1205 lbs of hay. $6.62 price. Very stormy this afternoon. Hay $11 per ton.

March, Wednesday 22. 1876.
Sleighing holds good. Father took 1875 lbs of hay to Auburn. He only got $9.00 per ton. He bought maple sugar.

March, Thursday 23. 1876.
Weather very fine. Thawed some. George Wilson's auction today. Not a very large crowd – things went cheap – generally barley 87¢ per bushel, oats 45¢ per bushel, spring wheat 25¢ per bushel. Cows $147, oxen $200 per pair. Seward had a pair there. 4-year-old horse sold for $100, hay $6.50 per ton.

We did not buy anything. We helped Hutson draw up two loads of wood. Pa drew a load of sand.

March, Friday 24. 1876.
Snowed some last night. I drew down 160 rails from the back lots to make a calf pen. Went over to Morland's sawmill and got 6 elm planks all sawed. Drew out 3 loads of manure.

MARCH, SATURDAY 25. 1876.

Went down to the village and traded waggons with Mr. Chase. We gave him our old waggon and $45. in Mason work for an other waggon and box he called the waggon $15. It rains to night

Mother, Rose, Father and I went over to Mr. Powell's this evening. Mr. Spaulding was down there. He is going to start west about the 10th of April.

March, Saturday 25. 1876.
Went down to the Village and traded waggons with Mr. Chase. We gave him our old waggon and $45 in mason work for another waggon. It rains tonight.

March, Sunday 26. 1876.
Snowed a little this morning. Ma wanted to go up to Grandpa's but did not. She and Pa went over to Uncle Jonathan's.

March, Monday 27. 1876.
Pa went to West Syracuse with Uncle Jonathan. Albert and I drew out 8 loads of manure.

Frank and Edd Powell came home tonight for a 6 day trip out to Dury. Pa came home on the 4:20 train. Weather about to freeze.

March, Tuesday 28. 1876.
Pa walked down to the Village to get the knives for the root cutters but did not get them. Mr. Huxford had not [yet] made them. Pa and Edd went to Jakob Waldron's to get the public money. P.C. collected 75¢ today.

I did nothing much but the chores. It rained quite hard tonight.

March, Wednesday 29. 1876.
Pa and I went down to the Village this afternoon and had George shod and got the knives for the root cutter. Stormy and rather cold.

March, Thursday 30. 1876.
Drew out 5 loads of manure this forenoon. Very stormy and cold afternoon. Mr. Powell has sold his old mare to Mr. Daniels.

March, Friday 31. 1876.

I drew out 8 loads of manure on wheat ground. Mr. Daniels and wife, and Mrs. Gardner and daughter visited here today. Mrs. Powell came over and spent the afternoon and Mr. Powell came over to supper. S---'s auction today. I have been over to Mr. Powell's this evening.

April, Saturday 1. 1876.

Father and I drew down an apple tree from the orchard in the forenoon. In the afternoon we went over to Morland's sawmill and got our elm lumber out of the way. There was 1533 cubic feet in all. It was sawed into 2-inch planks 2X4 and 2X6 and a few inch boards – it cost a little over $7.00. There is some birds-eye elm among it. Pa went down to the Village and drew the money or a money order for $50 from Mr. H. Colby we got yesterday.

April, Sunday 2. 1876.

Weather rather warmer than it has been for some time. I went over to Uncle Jonathan's. Uncle has a nice mare colt 3-years-old for $100. She is a light bay.

April, Monday 3. 1876.

Pa went over to Mr. Thompson's and paid him for Jim [horse]. Mr. Powell, Frank Powell, Pa and I joined teams and went out to Auburn today and came home in the rain. We went and saw the Centennial Reapers and Mowers at D. M. Osborn & Company shop. They were the Whalen No. 6 Combined, Burdick No. 4 Reaper, Buckeye Reaper, Kirby No. 1 Combined, with drop attachment. They were finished up to the handle, silver plated, and varnished to shine like chinaware. The Wheeler is the best in my eye as when reaping, the table may be folded the same as the knife bar.

April, Tuesday 4. 1876.

Weather rather chilly. Tinkered around home – did not do much anyway.

April, Wednesday 5. 1876.

Split 4 stakes to make portable fence. Attended Mr. Spaulding's auction

– did not buy anything. I got a few glimpses of Florence. Oh! What bliss. Went over to Mr. Powell's and had a first rate talk with Edd.

April, Thursday 6. 1876.
I did not do anything today on account of my lame back. Pa dug a ditch. I wrote to Fred K. Weather chilly. Went over to Mr. Powell's again tonight.

April, Friday 7. 1876.
Did not do much today either. Went to the Village. Mr. Powell bought a horse for about $175.

April, Saturday 8. 1876.
Father dug a ditch today. I done nothing but the chores on account of my lame back. Weather chilly. Got a letter from Uncle Sylvester [Tilscomb]- he has gone to Texas – 500 miles in a wagon.

His address
Rice, Navarro County, Texas

April, Sunday 9. 1876.
Quite warm and pleasant today. Roads very muddy.

April, Monday 10. 1876.
Mr. Hutson commenced digging ditch – Fred dug also part of the time. I went over to Mr. Powell's and helped Frank hitch up the new colt – his name is Jim. He took Mr. Powell's chest down to Mr. Weaver's. Edd and he is to work there. I built a bridge out by the barn in the afternoon.

April, Tuesday 11. 1876.
I cleared the rails off of the place where we are going to put the corn and drew them to put on our line fence by the O'Flaherty's. I plowed the garden. Father and Mother and Rose went over to Mr. Powell's. Weather very warm – lots of wild pigeons flying over.

April, Wednesday 12. 1876.
I plowed in the old meadow afternoon when it began to rain. I done nothing more – plowing runs good. I plow with the horses.

April, Thursday 13. 1876.
Plowed until the middle of the afternoon when it rained again – what ails the weather?

April, Friday 14. 1876.
Plowed until almost night when there came up a fearful shower. I got wet through – it rained fearful hard.

April, Saturday 15. 1876.
Pa went over to Thomas Gardner's to build a chimney. Bill Doherty came here and got a load of hay for Mr. Gillett. I plowed when I had time – rained some in the afternoon. Alex Turry Stuart [Alexander Turney Stewart] is dead – he was worth about $40,000,000 and about 70 years old.

April, Sunday 16. 1876.
Weather rather cool – went over to Mr. Powell's twice today. Frank Jones came up here and spent afternoon and evening. Fred Hutson came over a little while.

Pa went over to Uncle Jonathan's. Mark Browne had been down to Mottville. Cora is sick with scarlet fever.

April, Monday 17. 1876.
Weather very chilly. Plowed in meadow until noon then went to Village and got the blade sharpened. Broke the king bolt this afternoon – drew 3 loads of stone for stone ditch out in the south garden.

April, Tuesday 18. 1876.
Went down to the Village and got the bolt fixed – cost 10¢. Plowed in the afternoon in the old meadow. O'Flaherty's brother came over where I was at work to talk with me and he told me to tell O'Flaherty if he should ask me if he had been over where I was that he had not for he said O'Flaherty would horsewhip him if he found it out.

April, Wedneday 19. 1876.
Plowed a little for wheat but found it too wet and so plowed west of

the orchard. Father went over to Mr. Gardner's to do some work. Mr. Spaulding's people started at noon for Iowa. Oh! What made them go and leave me here alone. Weather a little warmer.

April, Thursday 20. 1876.
Plowed in the wheat lot all day. Rained a little at night. Weather rather mild. Frogs serenaded us tonight.

April, Friday 21. 1876.
Plowed all day for wheat. I plowed a good lot. Weather chilly and rainy. Mr. Jones told me 42 weeks time for cows was the usual thing though 9 months was generally calculated [gestation period]. Mooley's time up yesterday [Mooley was the family's cow].

April, Saturday 22. 1876.
Quite pleasant in the forenoon but rained in the afternoon. I plowed for wheat. I have about two days work more.

April, Sunday 23. 1876.
Rather dank in the morning but did not rain during the day. The red heifer "came in" - calf red heifer.

I went over to Mr. Powell's. Edd told me about the woman coming there to ------ and he saw her behind the house and she raised up her clothes. Frank Jones came here tonight. Mr. Durston's people have gone to Jacksonville to attend Mr. Durston's mother's funeral.

April, Monday 24. 1876.
I finished plowing wheat and corn stubble. Father went down to the Village. Mr. ----'s father is dead. Frank Powell is sick with toothache and swelled face. Spotted heifer's time up today.

April, Tuesday 25. 1876.
Rainy this morning - picked up stone in the clover lot. Albert Hutson helped me pick up stone - paid him with [an] old cart wheel Father went down and worked for S. Fields. Mr. Spaulding's people have been exposed to measles.

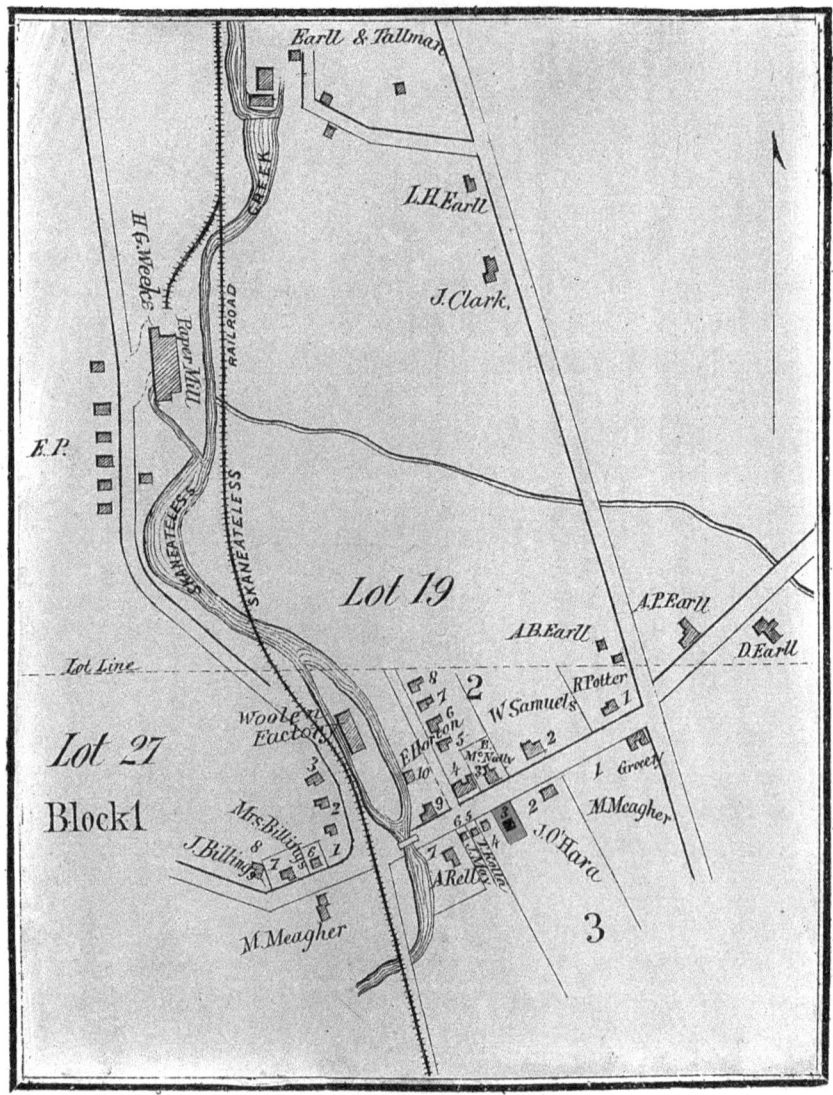

Willow Glen is just north of Skaneateles and south of Mottville. From *Atlas of Onondaga County, New York*, 1874. Steele Memorial Library, Elmira, New York.

April, Wednesday 26. 1876.
I plowed for wheat. Weather very fine. Will and Addie Durston spent the evening here. Mr. Fuller's funeral this afternoon - also George Ellsworth's mother's funeral. Mr. Jones has a sick cow. Hutson ditched - Pa painted wagon - 1 coat.

April, Thursday 27. 1876.
Plowed for wheat. Weather very warm. Hutson ditched. Pa painted wagon. I shot a cat with Edd's revolver in the kitchen chamber.

April, Friday 28. 1876.
Rained most of day. I did not do anything. Went over to Mr. Powell's this evening. Irving Rhoades was there.

April, Saturday 29. 1876.
Drew down some brush from the orchard – plowed, or finished plowing, wheat ground and dragged about an acre. Rained some tonight. Mooley "came in" tonight – her calf - red bull very large.

April, Sunday 30. 1876.
Weather stormy, snowy and cold.
We went up to Grandpa's. Stopped at Mr. D---'s a little while. Grandpa has 11 cows.

May, Monday 1. 1876.
Snow on the ground this morning quite deep. Plowed all day – finished the lot. The afternoon quite pleasant. School commenced today.

May, Tuesday 2. 1876.
Dragged for wheat all day. Weather quite pleasant. Watch tinker is here to stay all night.

May, Wednesday 3. 1876.
Finished dragging wheat ground. Went to Auburn and got 990 lbs of Lister Bro. Phosphate $17.66 also $35 cable chain. Weather very good.

May, Thursday 4. 1876.
Father went down to the plaster mill and got some plaster. Mixed 1 bushel plaster, 1 bushel ashes, and 2 bushels phosphate to make it. Sowed 3 acres of Western wheat in afternoon.

May, Friday 5. 1876.
Finished drilling wheat at 2 o'clock – 6¼ acres – 2 acres [of] China Tea wheat.

Helped Frank P. drill this afternoon. Sprinkled some today.

May, Saturday 6. 1876.
Drilled in about ½ acre wheat. Making 6¾ [acres] in all. Took the drill home. I quite did not like it much because it got muddy. Picked off a few stone and rolled the wheat. Father, Mother, and Rose went down to the Village – got package from out West contained a bed quilt, collar, napkins, cushion, and ring.

May, Sunday 7. 1876.
Weather warm. Thunder shower this afternoon. Frank Jones stayed the afternoon here – we pitched quoits.

May, Monday 8. 1876.
Weather fine. Plowed west of orchard and south of orchard. Rained in the afternoon.

May, Tuesday 9. 1876.
Plowed south of orchard all day. Pa went down to the Village. Rained tonight. Rose went over to Mr. Powell's all alone.

May, Wednesday 10. 1876.
Plowed ½ acre – sowed 2 acres of oats and peas and dragged them. It rained today – several different times. Went over to Mr. Powell's tonight. Edd's cow has a sore ankle and her ghumble [ungual?] joint is getting sore too. Her ears are like a piece of board.

May, Thursday 11. 1876.
Plowed all day. Father went down to Mr. Chase's and finished the mor-

tar. Weather pleasant but cool. Made a potato bin down cellar and put 15 bushels of potatoes into it from another bin.

May, Friday 12. 1876.
Rained this morning. Father white-washed for Mother and Mrs. Rhoades. We got 43 apple trees, and 2 pear trees from Edd Durston's and 2 or 3 plum trees from Mr. Rhoades. Sorted a few potatoes - cleared out the south cellar.

May, Saturday 13. 1876.
Drew a load of manure up to the orchard for the apple trees. Plowed all the rest of the time. Pa went down to Mr. Smith's on Franklin Street and plastered. Rained this morning and noon weather cool. Got red heifer calf from Mr. Powell for $1.00 – named her "Cherry."

May, Sunday 14. 1876.
Weather cool but pleasant. Made some phosphate for the corn. All the Hutsons and Jones came here this afternoon. We had a "regular backwoods Sunday."

May, Monday 15. 1876.
Rained some today. Pa set out trees in forenoon. Went and finished Mr. Smith's job. Rained all afternoon. Sorted potatoes and cut-potatoes.

May, Tuesday 16. 1876.
Drew out 4 loads of manure, 3 on garden, 1 on apple trees. Plowed. Weather warm. Went over to Mr. Powell's. Several gypsies went along tonight a-foot.

May, Wednesday 17. 1876.
Finished plowing south of orchard at 10 o'clock. Sowed it to oats – a little to peas – and got it nearly dragged. Windy, but rather warm.

May, Thursday 18. 1876.
Sowed oats and peas on big meadow – 4 acres - that I plowed this spring and dragged them. Went to the Village and got 3 bushel of peas. Weather warm and pleasant. Irving Rhoades brought down 2 lbs of butter. Got a letter from Uncle Sylvester.

May, Friday 19. 1876.
Pa finished sowing oats and I finished dragging them. Also dragged 4 acres of corn ground. I broke the dragger all to pieces. Weather very warm and pleasant. O'Flaherty threatened to shoot Fred Hutson tonight. I bet Fred was scared.

May, Saturday 20. 1876.
Weather very warm and pleasant – finished dragging corn ground. Talked with O'Flaherty's youngest brother (his name is Michael). I walked up to Rhoades's tonight. O'Flaherty and Mr. Hutson had a fearful time tonight - cussing each other up hill and down. Father got a 200 lb bag of phosphate today.

May, Sunday 21. 1876.
Weather warm. We fixed [the] fence all day. We turned the cows out today.

May, Monday 22. 1876.
Rained most all day. Father and I went down to the Village and worked for Mr. Chase. Albert Hutson went down with him. I mixed 9 wheel barrow loads of compost and 3 loads of ashes together for corn and potatoes. I cut ½ bushel of potatoes, shelled ½ bushel of corn and went up to Rhoades's a little while.

2 quarts of grated horseradish to a barrel of cider will keep it sweet and nice.

May, Tuesday 23, 1876
Quite cool this morning. I worked corn ground, drew out compost, and dropped it.

Frank Jones helped me mix 8 wheelbarrow loads more.

May, Wednesday 24. 1876.
Frank Jones and Mr. Hutson helped me. Frank and I dropped 14 wheelbarrow loads more compost and 250 lbs in a barrel and 200 in a bag and planted it. Pa has worked down to Mr. Chase's all this week. Mr. Hutson quit about 5 o'clock.

May, Thurdsay 25. 1876.
Frank Jones and I finished planting corn and planted about ½ acre potatoes. I went down to Mr. Weaver's and got a bag of Peerless potatoes.

May, Friday 26. 1876.
I planted ⅛ acre potatoes and drew out 5 loads of manure back of the barn. Weather warm and dry. Jim had a colt this morning – a bay mare.

May, Saturday 27. 1876.
I tried to plow but could not – the ground was so hard. I drew out 6½ loads of manure.

Weather warm. I drew down a load of rails for wood. Father has worked down to the Village all week.

May, Sunday 28. 1876.
Weather cool and pleasant. Father, Mother, and Rose went down to Mr. Deuel's today. The weight of Mooley's calf is 160 pounds.

May, Monday 29. 1876.
I plowed south of the barn. It rained very hard this afternoon. Thunder and lightning very heavy. I went down after father but missed him and he walked almost home.

Mr. Hill got the calves this morning. I mulched the young apple trees.

May, Tuesday 30. 1876.
I dragged, finished plowing, and marked east and west. Cold this morning. I planted sweet corn, beans, and two hills of squashes in garden. Mother and Rose went down to the Village today. Mr. Hutson dug [a] ditch.

May, Wednesday 31. 1876.
I planted potatoes today and a little corn. Mr. Hutson ditched today. Weather warm and dry. I went up to Mr. Rhoades's tonight.

June, Thursday 1. 1876.

Finished planting potatoes and sowed beets. Weather very warm. Mrs. Powell and Sarah came over here tonight. "Sally and I." I drew out 2 loads of manure for sowed corn.

June, Friday 2. 1876.

I drew out 8 loads of manure. Weather very warm. Irving Rhoades came down here this evening. Sprinkled some today. Johnny Elliott came and collected for service $3.00.

June, Saturday 3. 1876.

I took Father nearly down to the Village. Plowed for sowed corn. Rained in afternoon quite hard. Spent the evening at Mr. Powell's. Edd and Mrs. Powell went to the Village. Frank, Irving Rhoades and I stayed out in the barn until 10 o'clock. Irving said that Florence's uncle made her go out in the field and turn hay along with 4 men. Darned if I would not like to horsewhip that same uncle.

Edd and I are going to "haze" O'Flaherty.

June, Sunday 4. 1876.

Weather rather cool – rained some. I went over to Edd's quite a while.

June, Monday 5. 1876.

Finished plowing – dragged and marked – sowed corn ground. Fred Hutson works with me this week. Sowed corn in afternoon. Took Pa down to the Village. I saw Charley Abbott.

June, Tuesday 6. 1876.

Finished sowing corn. Mr. Gould and wife came here on a visit. Weather cool but pleasant.

June, Wednesday 7. 1876.

Worked on the road – self and Fred – half day. Father and J. E. Gould went to the Village.

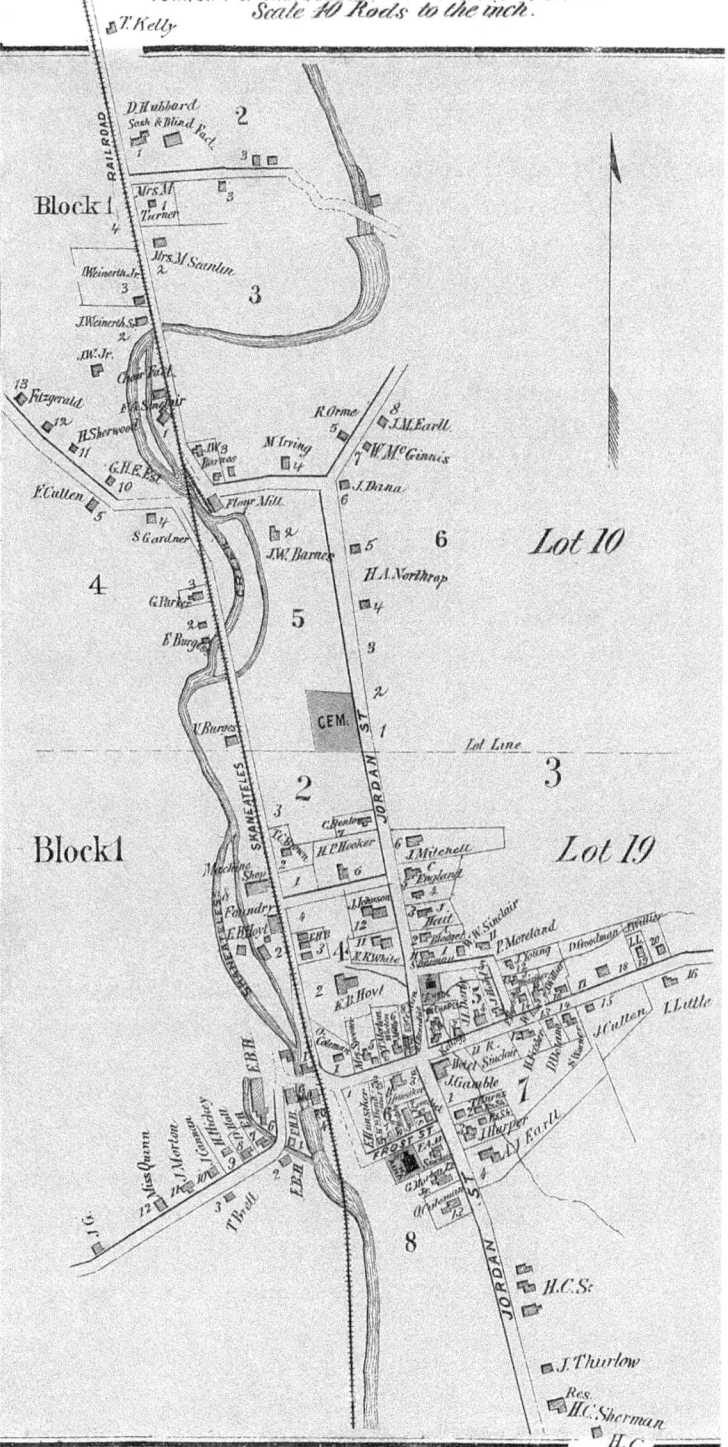

Mottville is north of Skaneateles. From *Atlas of Onondaga County, New York*, 1874. Steele Memorial Library, Elmira, New York.

June, Thursday 8. 1876.
Father took Mr. Gould and wife to Auburn. I made 2½ days work on road. Mr. Joseph E. Gould lives near Oshawa in Canada. Durham is his preference.

June, Friday 9. 1876.
Worked forenoon on road – one day gratis. Picked 2 loads of stone. 7 or 8 thunder showers this afternoon. Father took Edward's cow to bull at Scribbin's tonight. Continuous rain. Pa tore the flashing off of my bedroom today.

June, Saturday 10. 1876.
Rained some this morning. I tended mason. Pa plastered my bedroom. Albert and I picked up stone in back lot in afternoon. Pa went down to Mr. Chase's to work. I went up to Irving Rhoades's tonight. I received an "Illustrated Catalog and Price List."

June, Sunday 11. 1876.
Weather very warm. Father plastered my bedroom. I put 2 squares in my bedroom window.

June, Monday 12. 1876.
Weather very warm. I cultivated corn all day – forenoon with Jack – afternoon with George. Jack is a splendid horse to cultivate with. Pa went up the Frost place to work today.

June, Tuesday 13. 1876.
Cultivated all day with Jack. Weather cool. Finished corn one way – twice in a row and commenced the other way. Father came home tonight.

June, Wednesday 14. 1876.
It rained last night very hard. Thunder and lightning very fierce. Everybody was scared half to death. George shod down to Triphammer's [blacksmith] shop for 30¢. Went down to the Village this afternoon with 4 bushel of wheat – 52¢ for grinding. Got my hair cut down to the new barber 15¢.

June, Thursday 15. 1876.
Cultivated corn all day. Went to the Village at night with Mother and Rose. Weather very warm.

June, Friday 16. 1876.
Planted beans where the corn failed to come up. Sick all day. Weather cool.

June, Saturday 17. 1876.
Finished planting beans in corn. Cultivated some. Got load of rails for wood. Sprinkled some. Laid rails on the fence.

June, Sunday 18. 1876.
Rained most all day. I looked mowing machine over.

June, Monday 19. 1876.
Went down to the Triphammer's shop and got Fun shod. Bought hoe 15¢. O'Brigg's Circus and Managerie at Auburn today. Rained some. Mowed clover patch. Weather cool.

June, Tuesday 20. 1876.
Sowed a lot of turnip seed and cultivated, plowed, and hilled up potatoes. Rained some in afternoon. Mother, Rose, and I went down to the Village. Got letter from Jen. Got cucumber seed and candy for Rose.

June, Wednesday 21. 1876.
Took Edwards's cow to Scribbins's. Went up [down] and saw the boat [the *Glen Haven*] launched – she went off sideways as slick as a trout. Rained some – not much work. Planted cucumber seed.

June, Thursday 22. 1876.
Weather pleasant. Cultivated, laid tile, and filled ditch. Went to Willow Glen and got Aunt Jen. Cultivated in afternoon. Went down to Ogden's and ordered mowing machine knives. Paid Frank Jones 25¢.

June, Friday 23. 1876.
Cultivated, sowed corn and potatoes. Weather very pleasant.

June, Saturday 24. 1876.
Alexander and I went to Rhoades's to hoe corn, hoed ¾ of it or more. Mr. Wilson came and got his wood.

June, Sunday 25. 1876.
Rained like blazes today. Thunder and lightning, hail and wind. Aunt Jen and Mother went over to Uncle Jonathan's.

June, Monday 26. 1876.
Went to the Village and got George shod. Wrote to Mrs. Jas. D. Browne, Missouri for information about Texas.

June, Tuesday 27. 1876.
Put ashes on potatoes. Mother took Aunt Jennie down to the Village. Afternoon weather pleasant.

June, Wednesday 28. 1876.
Cultivated some, drew in hay, and mowed. Went down to Ogden's got mowing machine knives. Father came home.

June, Thursday 29. 1876.
Finished putting ashes on potatoes. Put Paris Green on the potatoes and garden. Raked hay.

June, Friday 30. 1876.
Spread out hay and drew it – in afternoon. Helped Frank P. get load of straw at J. E. Rhoade's. He helped me get in hay. Plowed corn and cultivated.

July, Saturday 1. 1876.
Put plaster on corn – got in raking. Rained afternoon. Went to Village and got fixed boots $5.00. I found one of them to be small when I got home.

July, Sunday 2. 1876.
Showers today and rainy. Temperature for water to scald hogs is 150 degrees.

July, Monday 3. 1876.
Took spotted heifer over to Scribbner's. Cultivated and plowed potatoes today. Weather pleasant.

July, Tuesday 4. 1876.
Rained afternoon. Not much fun at the Village. I went up [down] to Mandana and back on the steamboat for 25¢. Splendid ride. I saw Charley Milford today. Put Paris Green on the potatoes forenoon. Lots of fights today. Fireworks did not amount to anything – only a few skyrockets and wheels.

July, Wednesday 5. 1876.
Cultivated and plowed potatoes, hoed and mowed around garden today. Weather cool, rained tonight.

July, Thursday 6. 1876.
Put poison on potatoes. Plowed them a little, hoed a little. And cut meadow west of the house.

July, Friday 7. 1876.
Mowed around fence. Helped Jim Jones draw 2 loads of hay with team. He helped me in afternoon – cock hay and straw in 2 loads. Hutson got 2 loads of hay from J.L. Cliff with our wagon. Pa came home.

July, Saturday 8. 1876.
Got Hutson to help draw in hay 4 loads. Cocked up rakings. Headache [in] afternoon like everything. Very warm 90 degrees in the shade.

July, Sunday 9. 1876.
Awful hot 93 degrees in shade. Father went down to Junction and got William Carey. Fun is awful lame behind swelled ungual joint.

July, Monday 10. 1876.
Mowed most all day. Rained some in afternoon. Went to Village at night. Not much going on.

July, Wednesday 19. 1876.

A head ache
copious time
wheat all day
Took Moxley
to Scuffletown
before train
Went to village
to night with
Frank and Edd
Powell
Had some root
beer took currants
to ma. took pd
Calf died to night
father came home
He and I skinned
him

July, Tuesday 11. 1876.
Plowed up potatoes. Rained some today. Mr. H. Benedict drove in here with flour out of the rain.

July, Wednesday 12. 1876.
Cut hay forenoon. Drew 5 loads in afternoon. Went down to Village tonight. Weather very warm and sultry.

July, Thursday 13. 1876.
Drove white yearling to bull. Cut a little hay – drew in 4 loads afternoon all from lot south of the Hutson's.

July, Friday 14. 1876.
Drew in 2 loads of hay from clover lot. Cut some south of corn. Awful humid. Drew in 1 load south of corn.

July, Saturday 15. 1876.
Drew in 4 loads of hay. Cut some and got it in. Weather a little cooler. Old Andrew fell down stairs tonight at Eugene Rhoades's – hurt him some – he was drunk. I stayed all night with Irving.

July, Sunday 16. 1876.
Cooler today. Unloaded load of hay this morning.

July, Monday 17. 1876
Plowed up corn all day. Awful warm weather.

July, Tuesday 18. 1876.
Plowed corn forenoon – a little afternoon. Rained. Helped Mother wash.

July, Wednesday 19. 1876.
Helped Mr. Powell bind wheat all day Took Mooley to Scribbin's. Went to Village tonight with Frank and Edd Powell. Had some rootbeer. Took currants to Mrs. Huxford. Calf died tonight. Father came home. He and I skinned him.

July, Thursday 20. 1876.
Helped Mr. Powell bind wheat most all day. Rained like everything in afternoon.

July, Friday 21. 1876.
Cut [wheat in the] sandy lot. Awful cold. Mr. Durston drove 3 steers to Auburn. They ran through the wheat a little.

July, Saturday 22. 1876.
Raked and cocked it [the wheat]. 80 cocks. Chilly.

July, Sunday 23. 1876.
Weather chilly. Went over to Uncle Jonathan's a little while. Frank Jones and Sally are here. Had a splendid day with Sally.

July, Monday 24. 1876.
Cut back lot. Not much on it. Rained towards night – got wet. Pa raked and cocked some of it. Mrs. Huxford and Alley came here and picked some currants. Mother lent M--- Jones my binding gloves.

July, Tuesday 25. 1876.
Piled up rails down to the house and up in the pasture. Raked and cocked up more hay. Went down to Brown's and got one shoe on George. Fixed buggy and sulky. $1.80. Rained in afternoon.

July, Wednesday 26. 1876.
Took red heifer away. Helped J.E. Rhoades thrash about ⅓ day. 75 bushel winter wheat – 6 acres. Went to Village tonight. Heard Jed Irish and a man from New York were drowned yesterday.

July, Thursday 27. 1876.
Drew 5 loads in today. Weather cool and pleasant. Jed Irish and the man with him were capsized in a skiff by a squall striking the sail. The boat washed ashore and two hats were also found.

July, Friday 28. 1876.
Rained pretty much all day. Drew out 5 or 6 stowboat loads of manure on our clover patch.

July, Saturday 29. 1876.
Drew 1 load of hay in. Did not do much today. Father has started a hen house at the southwest corner of the horsebarn. They have recovered the bodies of J. Irish and Dalton today. Went to Village this evening.

July, Sunday 30. 1876.
[Cut] a little hay – drew it in at night. Father went down [up] to Elbridge today. Weather cloudy.

July, Monday 31. 1876.
Mowed some in orchard. Cocked it up. Mother, Father, and Rose went up to Jed Irish's funeral. Aunt May is going to be married in October.

August, Tuesday 1. 1876.
Finished cutting orchard and got it put up. Mother is not very well.

August, Wednesday 2. 1876.
Helped Mr. Clift draw in hay ½ day. Drew in hay from orchard. Helped Frank P. draw in two loads. Mother is better today.

August, Thursday 3. 1876.
Finished mowing along ditch – drew it in. Went hunting, Fred H. shot an owl. Hot.

August, Friday 4. 1876.
Got our lumber from Morland's sawmill. Sold some to Mr. Powell and Mr. Clift. Worked on hayrack. Hotter.

August, Saturday 5. 1876.
Worked on hayrack. Got some lumber from Mr. Clift. He threshed all day. More hotter.

August, Sunday 6. 1876.
Weather increases – more hotter.

August, Monday 7. 1876.
Hot – quite too hot. Cut wheat today. Frank, Edd, and Mr. Powell helped.

August, Tuesday 8. 1876.
A little cooler today. Finished cutting wheat. Helped Mr. Powell's people today.

August, Wednesday 9. 1876.
Helped Mr. Powell today. I was sick today – I did not do much.

August, Thursday 10. 1876.
Worked on hayrack forenoon. Helped Mr. Powell in afternoon.

August, Friday 11. 1876.
Drew in 14 loads of wheat. Edd helped all day. Frank, Mr. Powell, team and wagon - ½ day. Mr. Pearson's father from California came over here and stayed all night.

August, Saturday 12. 1876.
Helped Mr. Powell draw wheat. Father, my self and team - ½ day. Racked and drew in wheat – raking for ourselves.

August, Sunday 13. 1876.
Awful hot. Uncle Oliver came here from Uncle Jonathan's. More hot.

August, Monday 14. 1876.
Mowed oats and peas with mowing machine. Pa helped Mr. Powell ⅓ day. Mother, Rose, and I went to Village tonight. Raked and cocked some.

August, Tuesday 15. 1876.
Plowed oats and peas forenoon. William Sampson tonight went – crazy – I guess. Shouting and wildly swinging his arms. He is a file cutter in Auburn.

August, Wednesday 16. 1876.
Unloaded wheat rakings. Drew in 4 loads of oats – cocked up a few. Weather cool. Frank Powell helped unload 2 loads of oats.

August, Thursday 17. 1876.
Finished cutting oats south of orchard. Raked and cocked them afternoon. Pa went down [up] to Sennett [New York] with Uncle Jonathan to caucus.

August, Friday 18. 1876.
Cut oats up by the corn about 4 acres. Weather hazy. Mr. Powell helped us unload a load of oats.

August, Saturday 19. 1876.
Rained some last night. Mr. Jones threshed today. I helped. Drew the "Separator" up [down] to Lay Mason's about 4 miles from the Village on the East Shore Road. It was a pretty good draw for the team.

August, Sunday 20. 1876.
I hurt my thumb yesterday – it is awful sore. Cool today. Sally is down, also Frank Jones.

August, Monday 21. 1876.
Drew in 5 loads of oats – stacked them. Weather cool.

August, Tuesday 22. 1876.
Drew in 4 loads of oats – put 1 load of oats in the barn. Fred Hutson helped us.

August, Wednesday 23. 1876.
Unloaded oats. Plowed ½ acre with 3 horses. Hattie came here.

August, Thursday 24. 1876.
Plowed all day. Pa helped Mr. Powell thrash. Hired Ned Wilson to work in my place.

August, Friday 25. 1876.
Plowed all day. Pa borrowed a horse and took Hattie down to the Village.

August, Saturday 26. 1876.
Plowed all day. Weather cool. Took yearling to Edd Durston's.

August, Sunday 27. 1876.
Went to Village last night. Steamboat ran aground last night.

August, Monday 28. 1876.
Finished plowing winter wheat ground. Cool and pleasant. Went over to Mr. Powell's. Edd has 2 teeth out – he looks sick.

August, Tuesday 29. 1876.
Went to Village and got George shod – hind foot.

Plowed ½ acre in afternoon south of orchard. Awful hard plowing. Mulched a few apple trees in orchard.

August, Wednesday 30. 1876.
Rolled wheat ground today – it was a hard job. Father went to Auburn – got 2 plow points @ 40¢, 2 forks without handles @10¢. Got letter from F. L. Kilbourn today – he starts for Centennial this week.

August, Thursday 31. 1876.
Went cooning last night with some fellows from Auburn and Hutson's folks. Got home at two o'clock. Not any coons today to try the dogs – could not follow the scent. Dragged forenoon and drew out 3 loads of manure on wheat ground. Awful warm today.

September, Friday 1. 1876.
Drew out 10 loads of manure for winter wheat. Rain tonight. Kept the horses in the barn tonight.

September, Saturday 2. 1876.
Drew out 5 loads of manure. Made stack pin over at Mr. Rhoades's tonight. The thrashers have come tonight. Weather cool.

August, Thursday 31. 1876

Went cooning last night with some fellows from Canton and had one dog. Got home at two o'clock. Not any coons to day, the dogs could not follow them in. Bragged for now, drew out 13 loads of manure on to flat ground. Rained round to day.

September, Sunday 3. 1876.
Listen well and hear in mind
A virtuous maid is hard to find.
But when you find one good and true
Stick to her light with Spaulding's glue.
E.L.

Long may you live
Happy may you be
Blessed with forty children
Twenty on each knee.
E.L.

The rose is red
The violet blue
Lucky is the girl
That marries you.
E.L.

September, Monday 4. 1876.
Thrashed at J.E. Rhoades's today – Seward's horsepower.

September, Tuesday 5. 1876.
Finished at Rhoades's. Commenced at our job. Frank down just at night.
124 bushels wheat
69 bald [kind of wheat]
55 bearded [kind of wheat]
also 20 bushels oats and peas.

September, Wednesday 6. 1876.
Went to B---- show – the processional was not much. It was good in the ------ will have to finish some other time. Cousin Sam Gurnee from Wayne [New York] is here.

September, Thursday 7. 1876.
Drew out 8 loads of manure. Cool weather.

September, Friday 8. 1876.
Finished thrashing today.
Wheat 124 bushel
Oats 201 bushel
A little rainy.

September, Saturday 9. 1876.
Drew out 7 loads of manure.
Got Uncle Jonathan's 2 horses and cultivated.

September, Sunday 10. 1876.
Awful gloomy day. Awful lonesome.

September, Monday 11. 1876.
Drew out 3 loads of muck from woods.
Cultivated in afternoon. Bad cold and headache all day.

September, Tuesday 12. 1876.
Cultivated in forenoon. Dragged in afternoon.

September, Wednesday 13. 1876.
Dragged all day. Gathered quack roots [Canadian thistle] and burned them.

Stayed with Frank Powell all night.

September, Thursday 14. 1876.
Sowed a little wheat – ¾ acre.
Rained. Got spring to the drill fixed for 10¢. Stayed with Edd Wright – had a chat with Sally.

September, Friday 15. 1876.
Finished sowing wheat today. A little over 3 acres – 7½ bushel wheat, 800 lbs phosphate. I guess that will do.

September, Saturday 16. 1876.
Cut corn all day. Quite pleasant to day.

September, Sunday 17. 1876.
Awful dull day. Rained all day.

September, Monday 18. 1876.
Cut some corn. Fred Hutson helped. Sawed down a maple tree south of the orchard. Rained some.

September, Tuesday 19. 1876.
Rained all day. I did not do anything.

September, Wednesday 20. 1876.
Finished cutting corn. Laid stone walk to horsebarn.

September, Thursday 21. 1876.
Plowed most all day with two horses.

September, Friday 22. 1876.
Went to mill. I plowed all day. Quite pleasant. Saw a fight in Auburn today. Pa pulled most all of beans.

September, Saturday 23. 1876.
Went to Skaneateles Fair today. Pretty good show of tools. The Royce Reaper Company 500 weight took my eye – it is the neatest machine I ever saw or heard of. Several odd looking plows were on exhibition. Farmer's Friend, Champion, Buckeye, and Empire drills were exhibited.

September, Sunday 24. 1876.
Rained today – tinkered around all the forenoon.

September, Monday 25. 1876.
Cleaned up bearded wheat in forenoon. Frank Powell helped. Pa commenced his job on the bridge across the creek on Elizabeth Street. Job Weeks and George Haskins are partners – took job for $553.00 wages above the wages of $3.00 per day extra.

I finished beans – dug 30 hills of Peerless potatoes for ½ bushel.

September, Tuesday 26. 1876.
Cleaned up bald wheat in forenoon. Frank Powell helped. Rained this morning. I shot a wild pigeon in afternoon.

Had a few moments of delightful conversation with my "angel without wings."

September, Wednesday 27. 1876.
Cleaned up all the oats. Rained all day. Awful cold. Frank Foot stayed at the Centennial a week and he spent only $18.00.

Plow thistley ground in September.

[Cousin] May is going to be married the 9th or the 16th of November.

September, Thursday 28. 1876.
I guess it was rather pleasant today. Chored around most all day. Went to Auburn and paid N. Beardsley $31.50 interest.

September, Friday 29. 1876.
Rained most all day – fixed partition to keep Jack in the other barn. Picked up some apples.

September, Saturday 30. 1876.
Went to Village – had one shoe set on George. Got a pair of boots and pair of rubbers – but they are a little too small. Picked up some apples – drew down some wood.

October, Sunday 1. 1876.
Went over to Irving Rhoades's today. Charly is dead – died in the pasture. Went up again in the evening. Harwood came and Frank Hutson. I got Irving's "flagellator."

October, Monday 2. 1876.
Cut the sowed corn – drew in a small load. Weather cool but pleasant. Took Mr. Powell's mill home.

OCTOBER, MONDAY 9. 1876.

Dug potatoes &c
Hal - Ali - and
Addie came for 1-
a night.
Pkg came from
co. Delaware
co. Friday

October, Tuesday 3. 1876.
Dug potatoes in the forenoon. Fred Hutson helped [us] pick them up in afternoon.

October, Wednesday 4. 1876.
Drew off 55 bushels of wheat @ $1.00 a bushel. Went down to the rolling mill and got a derrick to use on the bridge. Did not get the chores done until 10 o'clock.

October, Thursday 5. 1876.
Got down some wood from the orchard. Wet and rainy – could not do much.

October, Friday 6. 1876.
Drew down 7 stalks of corn from the lot – husked some for the pigs. Rained today. Went to the Village this morning. Got George shod – hind foot. Got check on Skaneateles Bank for wheat $55.60.

October, Saturday 7. 1876.
Father went to Auburn and the rolling mill to see about the derrick. I made a corn crib but got it rather narrow.

October, Sunday 8, 1876
Cold and pleasant. 1/5 of horsechestnut grated in horse's feed once a day for 5 days and skip 5 days and then feed 5 days, and so on for a few weeks will greatly help and cure the heaves in horses and change them for the better.

October, Monday 9. 1876.
Dug potatoes – 6 bushels. Hat, Alex, and Addie came over at night. They came from Delaware County on Friday.

October, Tuesday 10. 1876.
Fred Hutson helped dig potatoes – 25 bushels. Mr. Brown came today. Alex, Addie, and Hattie went over to Uncle Jonathan's.

October, Wednesday 11. 1876.
Awful cold. Dan came here this morning and stayed till almost noon. Went to Auburn in afternoon.

Dan, Frank, and Henry 24 Washington Street.

October, Thursday 12. 1876.
Fred and I dug potatoes today – 4 bushels. Addie and Alex started for home. Carrie went over to Uncle Jonathan's. I had hoots of fun with her. She is just a little fast. She made a rag young-one and put it in my bed.

October, Friday 13. 1876.
Done a lot of chores – gathered 6 bushel of apples – very pleasant today. A flock of about 60 wild geese went south today

October, Saturday 14. 1876.
Drizzled all day. I picked up 3 bushels of apples. Done several chores.

October, Sunday 15. 1876.
Snow about 2 inches deep. I battened up the horse stable some.

October, Monday 15. 1876.
Drew down 22 stalks of corn. Got 1910 coal Cuddleback's $6.25 per ton.

October, Tuesday 16. 1876.
Worked at the apples today. Not much news today. I went chestnutting with F. Powell – did not get many.

October, Wednesday 17. 1876.
Worked at apples. Wheat bin sprung a leak – had to shovel some of it out into another bin.

October, Thursday 18. 1876.
Husked corn today. When I was not doing chores I husked 20 stalks [of corn]. Very pleasant today.

October, Friday 19. 1876.
Hutson and Fred husked today – 22 bushel. I husked 10. Very pleasant.

October, Saturday 20. 1876.
Rained some. Went to Village with corn for Johnny cakes. Fred Hutson down with me.

A modest girl wanted to tell her father about a jackass jumping over a precipice, so she said, "A Jackbottom jumped over a press water."

October, Sunday 22. 1876
Mr. Sessions and Susie came here today.

October, Monday 23. 1876.
Made my corn crib over. Husked a little corn. Very stormy wind today. Aunt Jennie came over from Syracuse tonight.

October, Tuesday 24. 1876.
Husked corn. Rather pleasant. Fred and Albert husked 7½ bushel of corn.

October, Wednesday 25. 1876.
Mother and Jennie went over to Uncle Jonathan's. I husked corn.

October, Thursday 26. 1876.
Husked corn today. Uncle brought Jennie over this morning. Rather cold.

October, Friday 27. 1876.
I took Jennie up to Grandpa's this morning. Cold. Got 2 squashes. Gathered some apples. Hurt my eye.

October, Saturday 28. 1876.
Stormy forenoon. Eye troubled me considerably. Drew down 32 bushels of corn from the lot.

October, Sunday 29. 1876
Stayed with Irving Rhoades last night. Eye very bad – cannot see half of the time. Cool but pleasant. Frost last night.

October, Monday 30. 1876.
Drew 2 loads of stone to the Village. Gathered some apples. Weather comfortable.

October, Tuesday 31. 1876.
Gathered apples all day. Quite warm and pleasant. Thundered today.

November, Wednesday 1. 1876.
Plowed garden and done numberless chores. Great Republican Parade today in Auburn. Hurrah for Hayes. Thunder shower quite heavy.

November, Thursday 2. 1876.
Plowed in the sandy lot today. 1050 horsemen paraded in Auburn yesterday. Warm and pleasant.

November, Friday 3. 1876.
Plowed today. Cool and cloudy.

November, Saturday 4. 1876.
Plowed most all day. Went down to "Republican Speaking" tonight. F. Jones, Fred Hutson, Jack Hutson and Father went also to speaking.

November, Sunday 5. 1876.
Pleasant today. Uncle and Aunt came over today. Had a private interview with her tonight – almost got caught.

November, Monday 6. 1876.
Got some wood from the woods. Went to Village with Mother and Rose. Awful windy. Saw Uncle Dan and Grandfather.

November, Tuesday 7. 1876.
Set up the corn that was blown down. Went up and got Miss Hattie Scribbins to sew for Mother. Went hunting in afternoon – did not get

anything – as usual. I shot at a rabbit and a chipmunk but missed both. Took Miss Hattie home tonight.

November, Wednesday 8. 1876.
I plowed this forenoon. Took the rest of Hutson's cider-apples over to Mead's cider mill (20 bushel). They have a steam engine to grind with – brought back 114 gallons of cider.

November, Thursday 9. 1876.
Plowed all day. Done a good lot. Hattie Scribbins has been here three days sewing for Mother.

November, Friday 10. 1876.
Plowed forenoon. Went to the Village and got the derrick and some boards.

November, Saturday 11. 1876.
Went down to the Village and drew off a lot of stone that was left from the bridge. Brought home the rest of the lumber.

Card Trick –
Take 21 playing cards and put them in three piles. Let some person choose one of the cards to himself and tell you which pile it is in. Then gather the piles up and put the pile with the chosen card in the middle. Then put in piles again...

November, Sunday 12. 1876.
...putting a card on each heap in turn. Let the person notice which pile it is in and gather them up again putting the pile that the "card" is in in the middle and then distribute them out again in piles as before. Let the person notice his card as before and again put the heap containing it in the middle. All this is done with the faces up. Now turn the backs up and count 11 cards. The eleventh is the one chosen by the person.

November, Monday 13. 1876.
Plowed all day. Warm and pleasant. School commenced in this district today. Fannie Beardsley [is] the teacher. Went down to Job Weeks [stone mason] and gave him $10.00 to pay Keenan for work.

November, Tuesday 14. 1876.
Rained a little this morning. Plowed most of day – almost finished the lot. Weather cool. Frank Powell came over a little while this evening. Tom Rice and his brother, Dick have gone to St. Louis to their brother's funeral.

November, Wedneday 15. 1876.
Went down to the Village and got Father's and Job Weeks's lime. Father fixed our side cellar way in afternoon.

November, Thursday 16. 1876.
Finished plowing south and west of orchard. Commenced south of barn – plowed there all day. Weather pleasant but cool.

November, Friday 17. 1876.
Plowed all day. Got old Jack into the ditch. Had quite a time with him. Went down to the Village [in] evening [by] horseback and got the mail.

November, Saturday 18. 1876.
Plowed forenoon. Dug some ground trying to find potatoes – succeeded in finding about a bushel during the afternoon.

November, Sunday 19. 1876.
Pleasant today. Father, Mother and Sis went over to ----s. I stayed with Irving Rhoades.

November, Monday 20. 1876.
Rained last night. Was going to help thresh at Jim Durston's today, but they finally concluded not to. I battened up the horse stable.

November, Tuesday 21. 1876.
Helped Jim Durston thresh all day. Cool and cloudy weather.

November, Wednesday 22. 1876.
Helped today also. Worked all day. Cool and cloudy.

NOVEMBER, FRIDAY 17. 1876

Snowed all day
Yet old Jack
in to the ditch
had quite a time
getting him
went down to
the village
Evening & got back
and got the
mail.

November, Thurdsay 23. 1876.
Went to Auburn today. I bought a watch at Smith's jewelry store. Waltham works – silver hunting case - number 898929.

November, Friday 24. 1876.
Snowed last night. I banked up hog pen. Father and Mother went to the Village in the afternoon. I stayed in the house with Rose.

November, Saturday 25. 1876.
Father, Mother and Sis went to Auburn today. I drew down 8 loads of corn from the lot and one load of corn stalks.

November, Sunday 26. 1876.
Went over to Mr. Powell's a little while. Went up to Rhoades's in afternoon with Frank Powell. Frank Jones and Sally were over at night. I went home with Sally. I won't write what was dared and done.

November, Monday 27. 1876.
Commenced going to school today. School not over full. Walked down and back. Walked over to Jim Roots to [see] Job Weeks in 15 minutes. Powell's people killed hogs today.

November, Tuesday 28. 1876.
Attended school, of course. The Prof is rather sharp – several new scholars.

November, Wednesday 29. 1876.
Went to school – studied hard but did not get any lessons.

November, Thursday 30. 1876.
Went hunting but did not get anything – too cold. Thanksgiving.

December, Friday 1. 1876.
Drew down corn stalks today Thermometer 4 degrees this morning – about 10 degrees at noon.

December, Saturday 2. 1876.
Cut down two small elm trees and drew them down. W. M. Kilborne came today – very unexpectedly.

December, Sunday 3. 1876.
Chilly today. Willis and I stayed at home all day. Sleighing today.

December, Monday 4. 1876.
Attended school. Will went down and stayed all day. The Prof is coming down on us this year. If we whisper – stay after school 15 minutes for first offense – 30 minutes second offense. More than 2 words [wrong] out of 25 [in Spelling] – stay after school and learn lesson.

December, Tuesday 5. 1876.
Attended school. Went with horse and cutter.

December, Wednesday 6. 1876.
Attended school. Went down with horse and cutter. Had pretty good lessons.

December, Thursday 7. 1876.
Attended school. Weather pleasant. Good sleighing.

December, Friday 8. 1876.
Attended school. As usual, quite pleasant.

December, Saturday 9. 1876.
Awful cold and blustery. 4 degrees this morning. Did not do anything except chores.

December, Sunday 10. 1876.
Cold but pleasant – thermometer 0 degrees. Read and studied all day.

December, Monday 11. 1876.
Cold but pleasant. Attended school – almost froze going down.

December, Tuesday 12. 1876.
Attended school. Organization of Literary Society this evening.

December, Wednesday 13. 1876.
Went to school. Everything very much as usual. George [horse] broke through the floor today at the Village. He went down straddle of a sleeper – his foot did not touch the ground.

December, Thursday 14. 1876.
Attended school today. Walked to school.

December, Friday 15. 1876.
Attended school. Speaking today. I did not have to speak.

December, Saturday 16. 1876.
Awful cold and stormy. Worked up some wood and shelled some corn.

December, Sunday 17. 1876.
Cold and stormy. Went over to Mr. Powell's and to George Rhoades's in evening.

December, Monday 18. 1876.
Walked to school. Pretty cold and stormy. Drifted some.

December, Tuesday 19. 1876.
Caught a ride part way to school – and had a ride home at night. Literary Society meets tonight. Stormy and cold.

December, Wednesday 20. 1876.
Attended school as usual. Nothing special going on.

December, Thursday 21. 1876.
Attended school. Pleasant, but not very good walking.

December, Friday 22. 1876.
Examination today. Arithmetic 9 to 10:30 – after that I had nothing to do so Frank and I loafed around all the rest of the day.

December, Saturday 23. 1876.
Killed hogs today. Frank P. helped – and Mr. Powell.

December, Sunday 24. 1876.
Loafed around all day. Irving Rhoades has got a watch for a Christmas present.

December, Monday 25. 1876.
Christmas. Went hunting [in the] forenoon and did not get anything. Not much Christmas for me - afternoon.

December, Tuesday 26. 1876.
Went down to Elbridge with Frank and Edd, to Edd's schoolhouse. Came back via Village. Cut up pork – weight 127 & 140.

December, Wednesday 27. 1876.
Drew some stone and fussed around.

December, Thursday 28. 1876.
Salted down pork. Father went to Village in afternoon – got 1 [bushel or basket] salt.

December, Friday 29. 1876.
Went up to Grandpa's and from there to Emmett's. Stormy. Arrived here [Emmett's] about 3 o'clock.

December, Saturday 30. 1876.
Awful storm – 20 inches of snow fell yesterday and today. Drifted considerably – awfully light snow.

December, Sunday 31. 1876.
Snowbound in Cream Holler [Cream Hollow Road in Niles, NY] at Uncle Emmett's and Aunt Mira's.

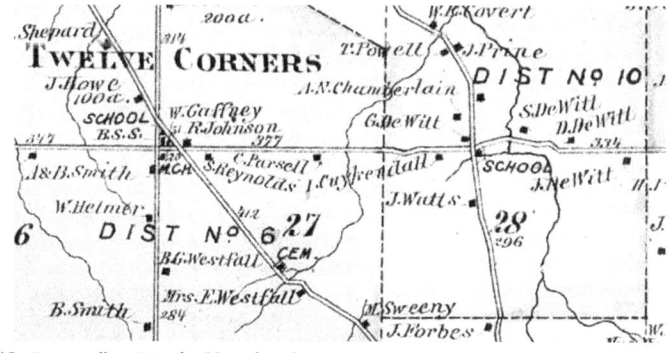

"S. Dewitt" is Uncle [Stephen] Emmett Dewitt. Cream Hollow Road is approximately 10 miles from Earll's house.

Earll K. Gurnee

Centennial Notes.

Jan. 1st 1876. The new year was ushered in with consider- able racket — in the shape artillery practice at midnight last night there were torch light processions head by bands of martial music. Cannon were also fired at noon to day

Great Centennial exhibition opens to day May 10th 1876

The Centennial closes to day November 10th 1876.

My height is 5 ft. 9½ in.
March 15th 1877

Centennial Notes

January 1, 1876
The new year was ushered in with considerable racket in the shape of artillery practice at midnight, last night. Cannons were also fired at noon today.

May 10, 1876
Great Centennial Exhibition opens today.

November 10, 1876
The Centennial closes today.

March 15, 1877
My height is 5 foot 9½ inches

Bibliography

Brinkman, Linda. "Soule Cemetery - Auburn Section." Rootsweb. Cayuga County NYGenWeb Project. 3 March 2009 <http://www.rootsweb.ancestry.com-nycayu,ga/cem/cem195_auburn.htm>.

Atlas of Onondaga County, New York: Homer D. L. Sweet, 1874. Steele Memorial Library, Elmira, New York.

Cayuga County Atlas: Walker & Jewett, 1875. Steele Memorial Library, Elmira, New York.

A thrasher, or mower, similar to what Earll would have used.

Afterward

Earll Kilbourne Gurnee is not listed among graduates of the Skaneateles Academy. He married the girl next door - Minnie Hutson in 1881. They had two children, Byron and Lulu Belle. Earll was listed in censuses as a farmer or a carpenter.

Minnie died in 1918. Earll died in 1944 on his family farm in his boyhood room. He is buried in the Soule Cemetery in Auburn. Byron ran the farm for many years after. The Gurnee house still exists on Franklin Street Road, just outside of Skaneateles.

Earll Gurnee's house today. Exterior and interior photogragrhs used by permission of Dwight and Laurie Wise, 2009.

Special thanks to

Elizabeth Batlle, Town of Skaneateles Historian
Pat Blacker, Skaneateles Village Historian
Dwight and Laurie Wise, Sennett, New York

More Publications from NYHR's
Learning from History series

A Darned Good Time (1868)
by Miss Lucy Potter

My Story - A Year in the Life of a Country Girl, 1880
by Ida Burnett

www.NewYorkHistoryReview.com

www.ingramcontent.com/pod-product-compliance
Lightning Source LLC
Chambersburg PA
CBHW051710040426
42446CB00008B/803